W9-DDL-148

Wellness Recovery Action Plan® (WRAP®) for Veterans and People in the Military

Mary Ellen Copeland, PhD

with assistance from Walter Hudson and Edward MaryRose Anthes

Peach Press

Publishers Note

This publication is designed to provide accurate and authoritative information in regard to the subject matter covered. It is sold with the understanding that the publisher is not engaged in rendering psychological, financial, legal, or other professional services. If expert assistance or counseling is needed, the services of a competent professional should be sought.

The <u>forms</u> in this book may be copied for personal use and as handouts for support group members. If any of the materials in this book are to be copied or used in any other document or in any other way – either in print, audio or on the internet - permission must be obtained in advance from Mary Ellen Copeland POB 301, West Dummerston, VT 05357.
Email: maryellen@svcable.net.

Copying and distributing portions of this book without citing the source is a violation of copyright. Copying and distributing this book in part or in its entirety is a violation of copyright, with the exceptions listed above. Sale of materials from this work without permission is not permitted.

ISBN: 978-0-9631366-8-8

Printed in the United States of America

CONTENTS

FORWARD

If you are on active duty, in the reserves, or have been in the military, you may be having a hard time coping with the hardship, trauma and loss related to military service and being involved in war-related activities. You may have feelings and symptoms that are extremely upsetting, that keep you from being the way you want to be and doing the things you want to do. In addition, things may be happening in your life that are difficult to deal with. Family members and friends who don't understand what you are experiencing and why you are behaving the way you are don't know how to respond or how to help. Some may try to help and others may turn away. You may feel like the situation is hopeless, that you will never feel well and enjoy life again.

A Wellness Recovery Action Plan must be developed by the person who will use the plan. If it is developed by someone else, it is not a Wellness Recovery Action Plan.

WRAP is for you and by you. You develop a WRAP for yourself if you want to. No one else can develop it for you-although you may ask others for ideas or to do the writing for you. You can do as much or as little as you care to with it. You can have long lists or short lists. You can skip some parts if you want to. It doesn't have to be neat. The spelling does not have to be correct. If you want to show it to others you can, but you don't have to if you don't want to.

The purpose of WRAP is to help you in the process of recovery, of getting well and staying well, and of assisting you in becoming who you want to be and making your life the way you want it. It will also be helpful to you in adapting to any challenges you have in your life like chronic illness, serious disability, being on active duty or dealing with extreme loss or grief.

You may want to read through this book at least once before you begin working on developing your own action plans for wellness and recovery. This will enhance your understanding of the entire process. Then you can go back and work on each section. You may want to do this slowly, working on a portion of it and then putting it aside and coming back to it at another time. After you have finished developing your plan, you may want to review and revise it on a regular basis—as you learn new things about yourself and ways you can help yourself to feel better.

This plan is based on empowerment and personal responsibility. It encourages you to focus on your strengths and wellness rather than on weakness and disability.

What is a Wellness Recovery Action Plan?

A Wellness Recovery Action Plan (WRAP) is a process that you use to develop a guide to assist you in working toward wellness, recovery and having your life the way you want it to be. It has become widely and successfully used in this country and around the world by people who have all kinds of physical and emotional health care issues, including veterans and people who are currently in the military. This book will guide you through the WRAP process.

The Wellness Recovery Action Plan works because:

- It is easy to develop and easy to use.

- It is individualized. You develop your plan for yourself. No one else can do it for you. However, you can reach out to others for assistance and support.

- It improves your ability to communicate effectively with your family members and health care providers.

- It directly addresses the feelings, symptoms, circumstances and events that are most troubling to you with plans to respond to them.

- It renews your sense of hope that things can and will get better.

- It increases your control over your life and the way you feel.

Here are the basic parts of a Wellness Recovery Action Plan.

- **Wellness Toolbox:** a list you make of simple things that help you feel better.

- **Daily Maintenance Plan:** what you're like when you're well, and a list of things to do every day to stay well.

- **Triggers**, and an action plan.

- **Early Warning Signs**, that things are getting difficult, and an action plan.

- **When Things are Breaking Down**, and an action plan.

- **Crisis Plan**, or Advance Directive

- Post-Crisis Plan

You can write your WRAP in this book. Or you can use a notebook or 3-ring binder with tabs for the different sections. Some people keep their plan on their computer, or use a tape recorder or digital recorder.

People who are using the Wellness Recovery Action Plan report that by being prepared and taking action as necessary, they feel better more often and have improved the overall quality of their lives dramatically. One person said, "Finally, there's something I can do to help myself."

Developing a Wellness Toolbox

The first step in writing your Wellness Recovery Action Plan is developing a Wellness Toolbox, a list of resources that you can use to stay and feel as well as possible and to use in difficult times to help you feel better quickly. When you think about this, you may be surprised at how many resources you have available to use. However, they may be limited due to your particular circumstances. For instance, your tools my be limited because you are on active combat duty or have a serious injury or disability.

On a sheet of paper write Wellness Toolbox across the top. Then identify and list those things you can use to help yourself feel better when you are having a hard time and to keep yourself well. Each thing on the list can be referred to as a Wellness Tool. Some of them are things you know you must do, like eating healthy meals and drinking plenty of water, and others are things you could choose to do to help yourself feel better. You can also list other ideas of things you could do or would like to try using to keep yourself well or help yourself feel better. You refer to this list for ideas when you are developing the sections of your plan. Some ideas for your Wellness Toolbox might include:

- eating three healthy meals a day
- drinking eight glasses of water
- getting to bed by 10:00 p.m. (or at a good, regular time for you)
- shaving
- getting a haircut

- doing something you enjoy – like playing a musical instrument, reading a good book, playing cards, watching a favorite TVshow

- vigorous exercise like running

- doing a relaxation exercise (simple exercises described in many self-help books that help you relax through deep breathing and focusing your attention on certain things)

- writing in your journal

- talking to a friend on the telephone

- email and IM

- getting together with a buddy

- taking medications

- taking vitamins and other food supplements

- hitting a punching bag

- taking a nap

- going to a support group

- taking time away from family

- working at something you enjoy

- taking pictures

- woodworking or some other craft

- fishing

- seeing a counselor

- meditation or prayer

- calling home

- getting cleaned up

You may also want to list things to avoid, like certain kinds of movies or videos, certain people, places, and activities.

You can get more ideas for your Wellness Toolbox by noticing the things you do as you go through your day, by asking your friends and family members for suggestions, and by looking into self-help resource books. Write down everything that seems good to you, from really easily accessible things, like taking deep breaths, to things you only do once in a while, like going fishing or seeing a counselor. This is a resource list for you to refer back to when you are developing your plans. Your Wellness Toolbox works best for you if you have enough entries so that you feel you have many choices, but just how many is up to you. If you feel positive and hopeful when you look at the list, then you may have enough. You can continue to refine your Wellness Toolbox over time, adding to your list whenever you get an idea of something you'd like to try, and crossing things off your list if you find they no longer work for you.

Once you've gotten your Wellness Toolbox underway, put the list in the front of your binder or put it at the beginning of wherever you plan to keep your WRAP. You can use the forms in this book.

Wellness Toolbox

You can list your Wellness Tools here.

_____

_____

_____

_____

_____

_____

_____

_____

_____

_____

_____

_____

_____

_____

_____

_____

_____

_____

_____

_____

_____

_____

_____

_____

_____

_____

_____

_____

_____

_____

_____

_____

_____

_____

_____

_____

_____

_____

_____

_____

_____

_____

_____

_____

_____

_____

_____

_____

_____

_____

_____

_____

_____

_____

_____

_____

_____

_____

_____

_____

_____

_____

_____

_____

_____

Daily Maintenance Plan

Part A. What I'm Like When I'm Feeling Well

Describe yourself when you are feeling all right. This may be a difficult task. With all that has happened in your life, it may be hard to remember a time when you felt well. If you can't remember or don't know how you feel when you are well, describe how you would like to feel. Make it easy. Do it in list form. Some descriptive words that others have used include:

- bright
- talkative
- outgoing
- energetic
- humorous
- reasonable
- argumentative
- ready
- successful
- competent
- brave
- courageous
- physically fit
- patriotic
- responsible
- loving
- religious

This list reminds us of how we feel when we feel well and how we would like to feel. It gives us something to work toward and reminds us that it is possible to feel well. It also is a good reminder that we can feel well and hopefully will very soon.

When I am well I am:

_____

_____

_____

_____

_____

_____

_____

_____

_____

_____

_____

Dreams and Goals. If you want to, you can use your WRAP to keep track of your dreams and goals. If you want to write yours here, go ahead. It will help remind you of what you are looking forward to. Then you can prioritize what you do each day so that you continue to work toward meeting your goals. If you don't feel like doing this right now, skip this section. Maybe you will feel like it some other time. Your goals might include things like feeling closer to your family, having a warm supportive relationshp, going back to school, getting a job that suits you, buying a home, stopping smoking, walking again, or being able to lift weights.

My hopes, dreams and goals:

_____

_____

_____

_____

_____

_____

_____

_____

_____

Daily Maintenance list. On the next pages, make a list of things you know you <u>need</u> to do <u>every day</u> to stay as well as possible and help you to get well and stay well. Use your Wellness Toolbox for ideas. Write these things down. Reminding yourself daily to do these things is an important step toward wellness. When you start to feel "out of sorts," you can often trace it back to "not doing" something on this list. Make sure you don't put so many things on this list that you couldn't possibly do them all. <u>Remember, this is a list of things you really want to do for yourself because you know they help you to feel as well as possible.</u> Don't give yourself a hard time if you neglect them from time to time.

Following is a sample Daily Maintenance list:

> • eat three healthy meals and three healthy snacks that include whole grain foods,vegetables, and smaller portions of protein

> • drink at least six 8-ounce glasses of water

> • take medications and vitamin supplements

- have 20 minutes of relaxation or meditation time or write in my journal for at least 15 minutes

- spend at least 1/2 hour enjoying a fun, affirming and/or creative activity, like watching a ball game, or doing some woodworking

- check in with myself: how am I doing physically, emotionally, spiritually

- go to work if it's a workday

- get some vigorous exercise

The things I will try to do each day to support my recovery and wellness:

_____

_____

_____

_____

_____

_____

_____

_____

_____

_____

Reminder List. On the next page, make a reminder list for yourself of things you might need to do. Check the list each day as you begin to use the plan to assure that you keep up with those things you might need to do. You'll avoid a lot of the stress that comes from forgetting occasional but important tasks. Write "Do I Need To?" at the top of this page and then list things like:

- set up an appointment with one of my health care providers or at the VA

- spend time with a good friend or be in touch with my family

- do peer counseling

- do some housework

- check on my benefits

- buy groceries

- do the laundry

- have some personal time

- plan something for the evening or weekend

- write some letters

- go to a support group

Do I need to:

_____

_____

_____

_____

_____

_____

That's the first section of the plan. Cross out items if they stop working for you, and add new items as you think of them. You can even tear out whole pages and write some new ones. You may be surprised at how much better you feel after just taking these first positive steps in your own behalf.

Triggers

Triggers are external events or circumstances that, if they happen, may make you feel upset, and you may begin to experience anxiety, panic, discouragement, despair, or negative self-talk. Reacting to triggers is normal, but if we don't recognize them and respond to them, they may cause us to feel worse and worse. This section of your plan will help you become more aware of your triggers and to develop plans to avoid or deal with triggering events, increasing your ability to cope and feel better quickly.

Identifying Triggers. Write "Triggers" on the second tab and insert several sheets of paper. On the first page, write down those things that, if they happen, might cause you to feel badly. They may have upset you in the past. It may be hard to think of all of your triggers right away. You may come to recognize more triggers over time. Some of them may surprise you. They may be things you did not suspect were triggers. Add triggers to your list whenever you become aware of them. When listing your triggers, write those that are more likely to occur, or which may already be occurring in your life. Some examples of common triggers include:

- flashbacks of traumatic experiences

- helicopters

- military planes flying low or fast

- seeing people with disabilities

- seeing people with particular kinds of features, of a particular race or wearing certain clothes

- hearing people talk in certain languages

- threatening behavior

- the anniversary dates of losses or trauma

- disappointment

- broken promises

- nightmares

- frightening news events

- too much to do, feeling overwhelmed

- family friction

- people letting you down

- people not understanding your situation

- others telling you what to do

- people drinking alcohol or people who are drunk

- people fighting

- a relationship ending

- spending too much time alone

- being judged, criticized, teased, put down or bullied

- financial problems, getting a big bill

- physical illness

- sexual harassment

- being yelled at

- being around someone who has treated you badly

- loud noises like explosions or shooting

- certain smells, tastes or noises

- particular kinds of weather

- roadside debris

- dead animals along the road

- someone driving fast toward me

List your triggers

_____

_____

_____

_____

_____

_____

_____

_____

_____

_____

_____

_____

_____

_____

_____

_____

_____

_____

_____

Triggers Action Plan. On the next page, using your list of Tools from your Wellness Toolbox, develop a plan of what you can do if your triggers come up to comfort yourself and to keep your reactions from becoming so serious that they disrupt your life and the lives of those around you. Include those tools that have worked for you in the past, plus ideas you have learned from others. You may want to include some things you know you must do at these times, and other things you could do if you have time or if you think they might be helpful in this situation. Your plan might include the following:

- take a few deep breaths

- check out the reality of the situation

- leave the situation

- watch a ball game

- do something I like to do that diverts my attention, like read a magazine

- go fishing

- play with children or pets

- get involved in a creative activity like painting or woodcraft

- make sure I do everything on my Daily Maintenance list

- call a support person and ask them to listen while I talk through the situation

- go to a support group

- do a half-hour relaxation exercise

- write in my journal for at least a half-hour

- pray

- play the guitar or work on an interesting activity for 1 hour

- talk to a buddy or a veteran

- ask someone close to hug me and hold me until I feel better

A successful way to use this list of triggers and action plan is to show it to your care providers and people who are close to you. Ask them for suggestions on what you can do yourself and what you can do with them or others to help desensitize you to certain triggers.

Triggers Action Plan

_____

_____

_____

_____

_____

_____

_____

_____

If you experience a trigger and you do these things and they are helpful, then great, keep them on your list. If they are only somewhat helpful you may want to revise your action plan. If they are not helpful, keep looking for and trying new ideas until you find the most helpful. You can learn new tools by attending workshops and lectures, reading self-help books and talking to your health care provider and other people who have had experiences similar to yours. The more accurately you can describe your triggers, the more effective you can make your Trigger Action Plan.

Early Warning Signs

In spite of your best efforts at taking care of yourself, you may begin to experience early warning signs, subtle signs of change that indicate you may need to take some further action. Early warning signs are internal, and may arise in reaction to stressful situations. Or they may just come up on their own and you don't know why. They are often overlooked or ignored. When you can recognize and address early warning signs right away, you can often prevent a much more difficult time. Reviewing these early warning signs regularly helps you to become more aware of them.

Identifying Early Warning Signs. On the first page make a list of early warning signs you have noticed in yourself in the past. If you have trouble knowing what your early warning signs are, think about how you feel when you know you are not feeling quite right, how you felt just before you have had a hard time in the past or when you noticed that your habits or routines changed. Your early warning signs might include things like:

- feeling anxious or frightened

- nervousness

- forgetfulness

- inability to experience pleasure

- lack of motivation

- feeling slowed down or speeded up

- being uncaring

- avoiding others or isolating

- being obsessed with something that doesn't really matter

- beginning of irrational thought patterns

- feeling unconnected to my body

- increased irritability

- increased negativity

- not keeping appointments

- changes in appetite

- restlessness

- pain

- thinking about drinking or using drugs

If you want to, you can ask your friends, family members and other supporters for suggestions of early warning signs that they have noticed when you are having difficulties.

Early Warning Signs:

LACK OF HYGIENE

LACK OF MOTIVATION

BECOMING DISTANT/NEEDY

WATCHING TU ALL DAY

AVOIDING FAMILY, FRIENDS CALLS

NOT SEEING A FUTURE

CONCERNED ABOUT FINANCES

SHORT-TEMPERE

Early Warning Signs action plan. On the next pages, develop an action plan for responding to your early warning signs, referring to your Wellness Toolbox for ideas. Some of the things you list may be the same as those you wrote on your Triggers Action Plan. If you notice these signs, take action while you still can.

Following is a sample plan for dealing with early warning signs:

> • do the things on my daily maintenance plan whether I feel like it or not
>
> • tell a supporter/counselor/medic/chaplain how I am feeling and ask for their advice. Ask them to help me figure out how to take the action they suggest.
>
> • peer counsel at least once each day
>
> • do at least three 10-minute relaxation exercises each day
>
> • write in my journal for at least 15 minutes each day
>
> • spend at least 1 hour involved in an interesting activity each day
>
> • ask others to take over my household or work responsibilities for the day

I also might, depending on the circumstances:

> • check in with my physician or other health care professional
>
> • go fishing
>
> • read a good book
>
> • listen to music
>
> • take a walk

Again, if you use this plan and it doesn't help you feel better, revise your plan or write a new one using your Wellness Toolbox and other ideas from workshops, self-help books, your health care providers and other people who have had similar experiences.

Early Warning Signs Action Plan:

• DO WHAT I DO NO MATTER HOW E FEEL

• CONTINUE TO DO WHAT WORKS

When Things Are Breaking Down

In spite of your best efforts, you may begin to feel much worse, but you know that you can still do the things for yourself that you need to do to help yourself feel better and keep yourself safe. You may have to "talk yourself into this". This is a very important time. It is necessary to take immediate action to prevent a much more difficult time or having things in your life get out of control. You may be feeling terrible and others may be concerned for your wellness or safety.

Signs that Things Are Breaking Down. On the first page, make a list of things that would indicate to you that things are breaking down or getting much worse. Some indicators for you might include:

- drinking

- using

- driving too fast

- yelling all the time, over small things

- feeling uncontrollable anger

- wanting to hit my partner

- increased nightmares

- increased flashbacks

- feeling very oversensitive and fragile

- irrational responses to events and the actions of others

1) ⊙ feeling very needy – GO DO# SOMETHING FOR ME IMMED-
   1ATELY
 • being unable to sleep

 • sleeping all the time

 • wanting to be totally alone

 • taking out anger on others

 • chain smoking

 • eating too much

 • not eating at all

Signs that Things Are Breaking Down

1) TAKE ACTION FIRST THEN GO TO WELLNESS
   TOOLBOX, DO AN ABC SHEET
   _____
   _____
   _____
   _____
   _____
   _____
   _____
   _____
   _____
   _____
   _____
   _____
   _____
   _____
   _____
   _____

When Things Are Breaking Down action plan.
On the next page write an action plan that you
think will help you feel better and avoid further difficulties when things are breaking down. Your plan

now needs to be very directive, with fewer options and very clear instructions.

Some ideas others have used for an action plan include:

- call my doctor or other health care provider, ask for and follow their instructions

- talk for as long as I need to an understanding person

- arrange for someone to stay with me around the clock until I feel better

- make arrangements so I can get help right away if I start feeling even worse

- make sure I am doing everything on my daily maintenance list

- ask for time off

- work more

- do deep breathing exercises

- write in my journal for at least half an hour

- write a long Email to someone I love

- ask for an emergency appointment with a counselor or care provider

- vigorous exercise

- go to a support group

- ask for leave

- call a hotline or warmline for support

This is just a sample. Some ideas may not work or be possible for you depending on your situation.

As with the other plans, make note of the parts of your plan that work especially well. But if something doesn't work, or doesn't work as well as you wish it did, develop a different plan or revise the one you used when you are feeling better. Always be looking for new tools that might help you through difficult situations.

If Things Are Breaking Down, I will do the following:

_____

_____

_____

_____

_____

_____

_____

_____

_____

_____

_____

_____

_____

_____

_____

Crisis Planning

Addressing difficult feelings and behaviors as they occur reduces the chances that you will find yourself in crisis. But it is important to confront the possibility of crisis, because in spite of your best planning and assertive action in your own behalf, you could find yourself in a situation where others will need to take over responsibility for your care. This is a difficult situation, one that no one likes to face. In a crisis you may feel like you are totally out of control. Writing a clear crisis plan when you are well, to instruct others about how to care for you when you are not well, keeps you taking responsibility for your own care. It will keep your family members, friends, care providers and buddies from wasting time trying to figure out what to do for you that will be helpful. It relieves the guilt felt by others who may have wondered whether they were taking the right action. It also insures that your needs will be met and that you will get better as quickly as possible.

Develop this plan when you are feeling well. Usually it takes a lot of time. You may want to collaborate with health care providers, family members and friends, other vets, and people at the VA as you work on this plan. The next few pages contain information and ideas that others in circumstances like yours have included on their crisis plans. It will help you in developing your own crisis plan.

The crisis plan differs from the other action plans in that it will be used by others. The other four sections of this planning process are carried out by you alone and need not be shared with anyone else; therefore you can write them using shorthand language that only you need to understand. But in writing a crisis plan, you need to make it clear, easy to understand, and legible to make it easier for the people you have chosen to use it. And while you may have developed the other parts of the plan rather quickly, this part is likely to take more time. Don't rush the process. Work at it for a while, then leave it for several days and keep coming back to it until you have developed a crisis plan that you feel has the best chance of working for you. Once you have completed your crisis plan, give copies of it to the people you name on this plan as your supporters.

A blank form for the Crisis Plan is included after this section. You can make a copy of it and then use the copy to write your plan. Then make copies of your plan to give to others.

Part 1. Feeling well

Write what you are like when you are feeling well. You can copy it from Section 1 of your Daily Maintenance Plan. It might help someone who knows you well to understand you a little better, and for someone who doesn't know you well – or at all – it is very important.

Part 2. Indicators that others need to take over for you

Describe those things you might do that would let others know they need to take over responsibility for your care and make decisions in your behalf. This is hard for everyone. No one likes to think that someone else will have to take over responsibility for his or her care. And yet, through a careful, well-

developed description of those things that would let
others know that you can't make smart decisions
anymore and may be in danger, you can stay in control even when things seem to be out of control.
Allow yourself plenty of time to complete this section. Ask your friends, family members and other
supporters for input, but always remember that the
final determination is up to you. Be very clear and
specific in your definitions. Use as many words as it
takes. Your list might include:

- being unable to recognize or correctly identify family members and friends

- uncontrollable pacing, unable to stay still

- neglecting personal hygiene (for how many
days?)

- not cooking or doing any housework (for
how many days?)

- not understanding what people are saying

- thinking I am someone I am not

- thinking I have the ability to do something
I don't

- abusive, destructive or violent behavior,
toward self, others, or property
- substance abuse
- not getting out of bed (for how long?)
- hitting people
- refusing to eat or drink
- extreme rage
- frightening or threatening other people

Part 3. Supporters

In this next section of the crisis plan, list those people who you want to take over for you if they notice these indicators. Before listing someone in this part of your plan, talk with them about what you'd like from them and make sure they understand and agree to be in the plan. They can be family members, buddies, other people who have had experiences similar to yours, or health care providers. They should be committed to following the plans you have written. As you work on developing your support system, try to change the list so you rely more heavily on family members, friends, and people who have had experiences similar to yours and less on care providers, who may not be available when you need them.

It's a good idea to have at least five people on your list of supporters. If you have only one or two, they might not be available when you really need them, like when they are deployed or reassigned, go on leave or are sick. If you don't have that many supporters now, you may need to work on developing new and/or closer relationships with people. Ask yourself how best you can build these kinds of relationships.

There may be people who have made decisions that were not according to your wishes in the past and whom you do not want involved in your care again. Write on your plan, "I do not want the following people involved in any way in my care or treatment," and then list those people and why you don't want them involved. They may be people who have treated you badly in the past, have made poor decisions in your behalf, or who get too upset when you are having a hard time.

Many people like to include a section that describes how they want possible disputes between their supporters settled. For instance, you may want to say that if there is any disagreement about a course of action, a majority of your supporters can decide, or that a particular person will make the determination. Or you might want a person who has had experiences similar to yours, or a military advocacy group, to be involved in the decision-making.

Part 4. Health care providers and medications

Name your physician, pharmacist and other health care and insurance providers, along with their phone numbers. Then list:

> • the medications you are currently using, the dosage and why you are using them,

> • those medications you would prefer to take if medications or additional medications became necessary – like those that have worked well for you in the past – and why you would choose them,

> • those medications that would be acceptable to you if medications became necessary and why you would choose them, and

> • those medications that must be avoided – like those you are allergic to, that conflict with another medication or cause undesirable side effects – and give the reasons they should be avoided.

Also list any vitamins, herbs, alternative medications (such as homeopathic remedies) and supplements you are taking, which to increase or decrease if you are in crisis, and which you have discovered are not good for you.

Part 5. Treatments

There may be particular treatments that you would like in a crisis situation and others that you would want to avoid. The reason may be as simple as "this treatment has or has not worked in the past," or you may have some concerns about the safety of this treatment, or maybe you just don't like the way it makes you feel. Treatments here can mean medical procedures or the many possibilities of alternative therapy, such as injections of B vitamins, massages, or cranial sacral therapy. In this part of your crisis plan, list:

> • any treatments you are currently undergoing and why,

> • those treatments you would prefer if treatments or additional treatments became necessary and why you would choose them,

> • those treatments that would be acceptable to you if treatments were deemed necessary by your support team, and

> • those treatments that must be avoided and why.

Part 6. Planning for your care

Describe a plan for your care in a crisis that would allow you to stay at home, in your community, or stay part-time at home and part-time in the community. Think about your family and friends. Would they be able to take turns providing you with care? Could transportation be arranged to health care appointments? Is there a program in your community that could provide you with care part of the time, with family members and friends taking care of you the rest of the time? Many people who would prefer to stay at home rather than being hospitalized are setting up these kinds of plans. You may need to ask your family members, friends and health care providers what options are available. If you are having a hard time coming up with a plan, at least write down what you imagine the ideal scenario would be.

Part 7. Treatment facilities

Describe the treatment facilities you would like to use if family members and friends cannot provide you with care, or if your condition requires special care. Your options may be limited by the facilities that are available in your area, your insurance coverage and other benefits you may be receiving. If you are not sure which facilities you would like to use, write down a description of what the ideal facility would be like. Then talk to family members and friends about the available choices and call the facilities to request information that may help you in making a decision. Also include a list of treatment facilities you would like to avoid – such as places where you received poor care in the past.

Part 8. What you need from others

Describe what your supporters can do for you that will help you feel better. This part of the plan is very important and deserves careful attention. Describe anything you can think of that you want your supporters to do (or not do) for you to help you feel more comfortable. You may want to get more ideas from your supporters and health care professionals.

Some things others could do for you that would help you feel better might include:

- listen to me without giving me advice, judging me or criticizing me

- just stay with me

- validate what I am experiencing

- do whatever you need to do to keep me and others safe

- hold me (how? how firmly?)

- don't touch me

- let me pace

- encourage me to move, help me move

- provide me with materials so I can draw or paint

- give me the space to express my feelings

- don't talk to me (or, do talk to me)

- encourage me and reassure me

- feed me nutritious food

- make sure I take my vitamins and other medications

- play me comic videos

- play me good music (list the kind)

- just let me rest

- help me excercise

Include a list of specific tasks you would like others to do for you, who you would like to do which task, and any specific instructions they might need. These tasks might include:

- cooking
- cleaning up
- buying groceries
- feeding the pets
- taking care of the children
- paying the bills
- taking out the trash
- doing the laundry

You may also want to include a list of things that you do not want others to do for you – things they might otherwise do because they think it would be helpful, but that might even be harmful or worsen the situation. These might include:

- forcing you to do anything – such as walking
- scolding you
- becoming impatient with you
- taking away your cigarettes or coffee
- talking continuously
- involuntary restraint or seclusion

Some people also include instructions in this section on how they want to be treated by those taking over their care. These instructions might include statements such as "kindly but firmly tell me what you are going to do," "don't ask me to make any choices at this point," or "take my medications out of my top dresser drawer right away and hide them."

Part 9. Recognizing recovery

In the last part of this plan, give your supporters information on how to recognize when you have recovered enough so that you can take care of yourself and so that they no longer need to use this plan. Some examples include:

- when I am eating at least two meals a day

- when I am awake for six hours a day

- when I am taking care of my personal hygiene needs daily

- when I can carry on a good conversation

- when I can easily walk around the house

- when I stop threatening to harm myself or others

- when I know where I am and what I am doing

This is your crisis plan. Update it when you learn new information or change your mind about things. Date your crisis plan each time you change it and give revised copies to your supporters.

You can help assure that your crisis plan will be followed by signing it in the presence of two witnesses. It will further increase its potential for use if you appoint and name a durable power of attorney – a person who could legally make decisions for you if you were not able to make them for yourself. Since the legality of these documents varies from state to state, you cannot be absolutely sure the plan will be followed. However, it is your best assurance that your wishes will be honored.

Personal Crisis Plan
To be used if the circumstances described in part 2 of this document occur.

Mary Ellen Copeland
PO Box 301,   West Dummerston, VT 05357
Phone: (802) 254-2092   Fax: (802) 257-7449
copeland@mentalhealthrecovery.com
www.mentalhealthrecovery.com

Name _____

Date _____

Part 1 What I'm like when I'm feeling well.

_____
_____
_____
_____
_____
_____
_____
_____
_____
_____
_____
_____
_____
_____
_____
_____
_____
_____
_____
_____
_____
_____
_____

_____

_____

_____

_____

_____

_____

Part 2 Symptoms

If I have several of the following signs and/or symptoms, my supporters, named on the next page, need
to take over responsibility for my care and make
decisions in my behalf based on the information in
this plan.

_____

_____

_____

_____

_____

_____

_____

_____

_____

_____

_____

_____

_____

_____

_____

_____

_____

_____

_____

_____

_____

Part 3 Supporters

If this plan needs to be activated, I want the following people to take over for me.

Name   **Connection/role**   **Phone #**
_____

Specific Tasks for this Person
_____
_____
_____

Name   **Connection/role**   **Phone #**
_____

Specific Tasks for this Person
_____
_____
_____

Name   **Connection/role**   **Phone #**
_____

Specific Tasks for this Person
_____
_____
_____

Name   **Connection/role**   **Phone #**
_____

Specific Tasks for this Person
_____
_____
_____

Name   **Connection/role**   **Phone #**

_____

Specific Tasks for this Person

_____

_____

_____

<u>I do not</u> want the following people involved in any way in my care or treatment:

Name_____

I don't want them involved because: (optional)

_____

Name_____

I don't want them involved because: (optional)

_____

Name_____

I don't want them involved because: (optional)

_____

Name_____

I don't want them involved because: (optional)

_____

Settling Disputes Between Supporters
If my supporters disagree on a course of action to be followed, I would like the dispute to be settled in the following way:

_____

_____

_____

_____

Part 4 Medications / Supplements / Health Care Preparations:

Physician_____

Psychiatrist_____

Other Health Care Providers

_____

_____

_____

_____

Pharmacy_____

Pharmacist_____

Allergies_____

_____

Insurance

Information_____

_____

Medication / Supplement / Health Care Preparation
   Dosage

_____

Purpose_____

Medication / Supplement / Health Care Preparation
   Dosage

_____

Purpose_____

Medication / Supplement / Health Care Preparation
   Dosage

_____

Purpose_____

Medication / Supplement / Health Care Preparation
   Dosage

_____

Purpose_____

Medication / Supplement / Health Care Preparation
        Dosage
_____

Purpose_____

Medication / Supplement / Health Care Preparation
        Dosage
_____

Purpose_____

Medication / Supplement / Health Care Preparation
        Dosage
_____

Purpose_____

Medication / Supplement / Health Care Preparation
        Dosage
_____

Purpose_____

Medication / Supplement / Health Care Preparation
        Dosage
_____

Purpose_____

Medication / Supplement / Health Care Preparation
        Dosage
_____

Purpose_____

Medication / Supplement / Health Care Preparation
        Dosage
_____

Purpose_____
Medication / Supplement / Health Care Preparation
        Dosage
_____

Purpose_____

** Medications / Supplements / Health Care Preparations to Avoid **

Why?

_____
_____
_____
_____
_____
_____

take special note

Part 5   *Treatments and Complementary Therapies*

Treatment/Complementary Therapy

_____

When and how to use this treatment/complementary therapy

_____
_____
_____

Treatment/Complementary Therapy

_____

When and how to use this treatment/complementary therapy

_____
_____
_____

Treatment/Complementary Therapy

_____

When and how to use this treatment/complementary therapy

_____

_____

_____

Treatment/Complementary Therapy

_____

When and how to use this treatment/complementary
therapy

_____

_____

_____

Part 6 Home Care / Community Care / Respite Center

If possible, follow this care plan:

_____

_____

_____

_____

_____

_____

_____

_____

_____

_____

_____

_____

_____

_____

_____

_____

_____

_____

_____

_____

_____

_____

Part 7 Hospital or other Treatment Facilities

If I need hospitalization or treatment in a treatment facility, I prefer the following facilities in order of preference

Name_____
Contact Person_____
Phone Number_____
I prefer this facility because

_____

Name_____
Contact Person_____
Phone Number_____
I prefer this facility because

_____

Name_____
Contact Person_____
Phone Number_____
I prefer this facility because

_____

Name_____
Contact Person_____
Phone Number_____
I prefer this facility because

_____

Avoid using the following hospital or treatment facilities

Name   Reason to avoid using

_____
_____
_____
_____

Part 8 Help from others

Please do the following things that would help reduce my symptoms, make me more comfortable and keep me safe.

_____
_____
_____
_____
_____
_____
_____
_____
_____
_____
_____
_____
_____
_____
_____
_____
_____
_____
_____
_____
_____
_____
_____
_____

I need (name the person) _____ to (task)_____
_____

I need (name the person) _____ to (task)_____
_____

I need (name the person) _____ to
(task)_____

_____

I need (name the person) _____ to
(task)_____

_____

I need (name the person) _____ to
(task)_____

_____

I need (name the person) _____ to
(task)_____

_____

I need (name the person) _____ to
(task)_____

_____

I need (name the person) _____ to
(task)_____

_____

**Do not do the following. It won't help and it
may even make things worse.**

_____
_____
_____
_____
_____
_____
_____
_____
_____
_____
_____

Part 9 Inactivating the Plan

The following signs, lack of symptoms or actions
indicate that my supporters no longer need to use
this plan.

_____

_____

_____

_____

_____

_____

_____

_____

_____

I developed this plan on (date) _____ with
the help of _____

Any plan with a more recent date supersedes this
one.

Signed_____Date_____

Witness_____Date_____

Witness_____Date_____

Attorney_____Date_____

Durable Power of

Attorney_____

Substitute for Durable Power of Attorney

_____

**Any Personal Crisis Plan developed on a date
after the dates listed above takes precedence
over this document.**

Post Crisis Plan

That time after you have had a very difficult time and when you are working toward feeling good again can be very difficult. Others may assume you are still having difficulties and try to control you. You may not trust your own feelings and behaviors. You may be feeling very discouraged. Thinking about this possibility before you have any difficulties, when you are feeling alright, can make it easier for you to recover from a crisis.

You may want to think about some of the following issues and even write some notes that will guide you when you are working to get over a difficult time.

How will I know, and how will my supporters know, that I am doing well enough to think about my recovery?

Who will I want to support me through this time?

What are some things I might need to do as soon as I start feeling better?

What can I ask others to do for me?

What are some things that can wait until I feel better?

What do I need to do for myself every day while I am getting over this difficult time?

What things and people do I need to avoid?
What signs would show me that I may be beginning to feel worse?

What Wellness Tools will I use if I am starting to feel worse?

What might I need to do to prevent further repercussions from this crisis--and when will I do these things?

Who are the people I might need to thank?

Who are people I might need to apologize to?

When and how might I do that?

Who are people I might need to make amends with and when and how will I do that?

What possible medical, legal, or financial issues might need to be resolved and how will I do that?

What might I need to do to prevent further loss?

How will I know when this post crisis phase is over and I can return to using my Daily Maintenance Plan as my guide to things to do for myself every day?

Are there any changes in the first four sections of my Action Plans for Prevention and Recovery that might help prevent such a crisis in the future?

Is there anything in my crisis plan I might need to change?

What did I learn from this crisis?

Are there changes I want to make in my lifestyle or life goals?

Using Your Action Plans

You have now completed your Wellness Recovery Action Plan. At first you will need to spend 15 or 20 minutes each day reviewing your plans. People report that the morning, either before or after breakfast, is the best time to review the plan. As you become familiar with your Daily Maintenance list, Triggers, indicators of difficulties and response plans, you will find that the review process takes less time and that you will know how to respond without even referring your plan.

Begin with Section 1. Review the list of how you are when you are feeling well. If you are all right, do the things on your list of things you need to do every day to keep yourself well. Also refer to the page of things you may need to do to see if there is anything you need to do that day. If there is, make a note to yourself to include it in your day. If you are not feeling all right, review the other sections to see where how you are feeling fits in. Then follow your action plan.

For instance, if you feel very anxious and know that it is because one of your triggers happened, follow the plan in the triggers section. If there weren't any particular triggers but you noticed some early warning signs, follow the plan you designed for that section. If you feel like things have gotten much worse, follow the plan you developed there.

If you are in a crisis situation, the plans will help you to realize that so you can let your supporters know you need assistance. However, in certain crisis situations, you may not be aware or willing to admit that you are in crisis. This is why having a strong team of supporters is so important. They will observe the indicators you have reported and take over responsibility for your care, whether or not you are willing to admit you are in a crisis at that time. Distributing your crisis plan to your supporters and discussing it with them is key to your safety and well being.

Considering the post crisis plan or your responses to those issues from time to time will help you be better prepared in case you need to use that part of the plan at some time.

You may want to consider taking your plan or parts of your plan to the copy shop and having a copy made that is reduced in size so you can easily carry it in your pocket, purse or glove compartment. Then you can refer to the plan if triggers or symptoms come up when you are away from home.

People who are using these plans regularly and updating them as necessary are finding that they have fewer difficult times, and that when they do have a hard time it is not as bad as it used to be and it doesn't last as long.

I hope this book has been helpful to you. Special thanks to you for all the good work you have done and the sacrifices you have made. Please know that you are a worthy person who deserves all the best that life has to offer.

Mary Ellen Copeland

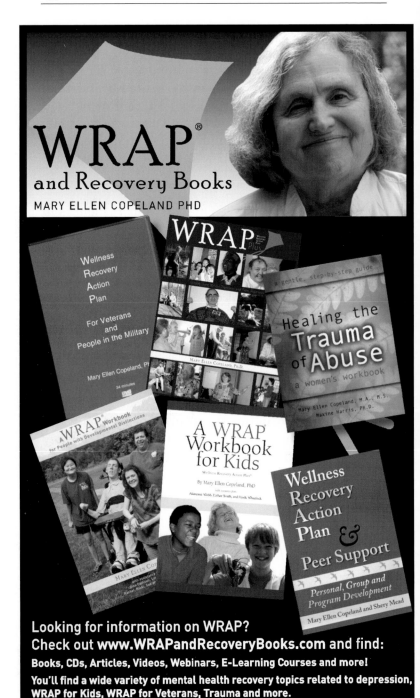

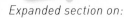

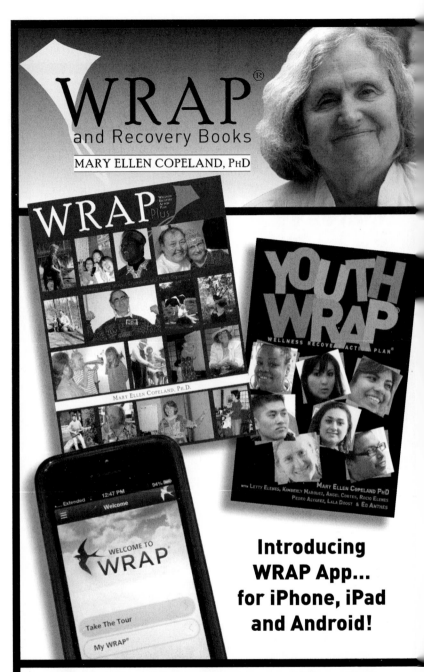